Ann Wilson Adult Coloring Book

Lead Singer of the Heart and Rock Diva, Dramatic Soprano Voice and Talent Inspired Adult Coloring Book

Robin Larsen

cher

THERE IS A SONG
THE RIVER SINGS,
THERE IS A RIVER
SINGS YOUR NAME,
THE AIR IS LIVING
HUMMING
THE SLANTING SUN
IN HEAVEN'S VIEW
HEART
"HEAVEN"
BEAUTIFUL BROKEN

ANN WILSON

.com
the next best thing to being there

Ann Wilson

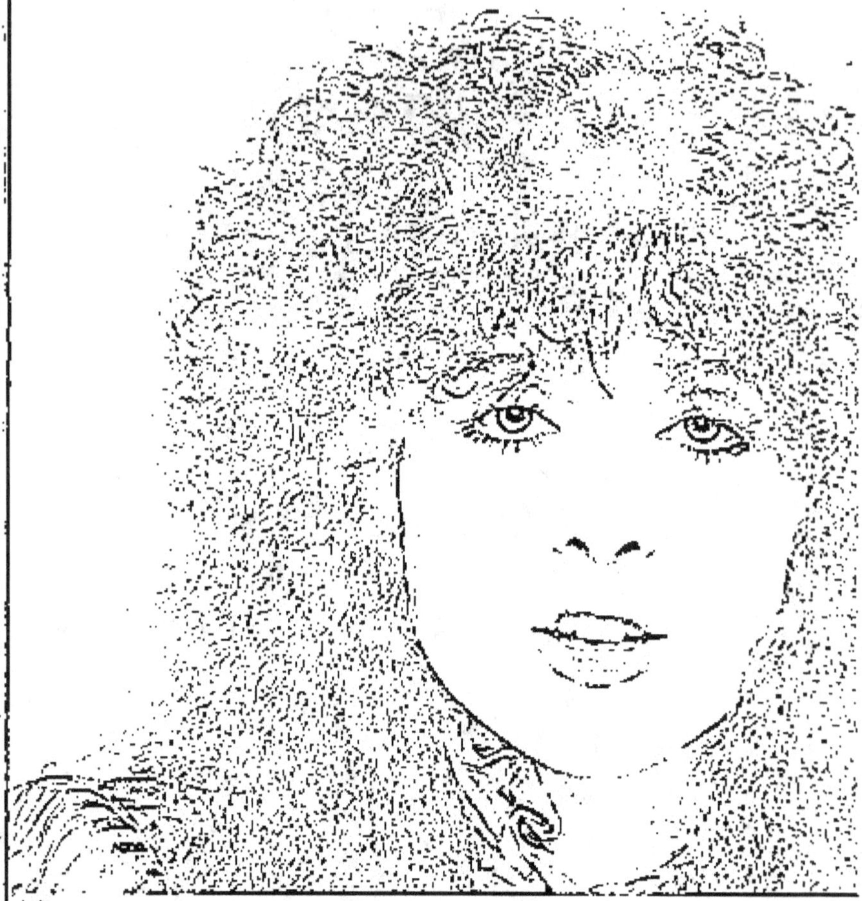

Chinatown, featuring future Heart guitarist Howard Leese.

Mushroom/Can Base studio was manned by Los Angeles-born record producer Mike Flicker and his engineer, the aforementioned Howard Leese (also from Los Angeles and also a one-time member of psych band The Zoo), and their plan was to sign and develop new acts. Mike Fisher got wind of the situation and approached the studio about Heart. They liked what they heard; however, Mushroom was only interested in signing vocalist Ann.

Ann insisted that they work with the whole group or not at all, so Mushroom decided to pass. However, a year later the label again approached the band with a fresh offer, a two-album contract to be recorded at Mushroom by in-house producer Mike Flicker. It wasn't a great deal, but at least it was a step forward.

The band quickly recorded a series of tracks including the mystical *How Deep It Goes*, along with the epic *Crazy On You*, the powerful *Magic Man*, the dreamy *Soul Of The Sea*, and *Dreamboat Annie*, which would later become the centrepiece of the group's 1976 debut album of the same name.

"That song was originally like a Beach Boys thing, a California Calypso-type vibe," notes Ann. "It wasn't supposed to be in reference to me – it was just a random name, because it fit the groove. The lyric then started to lead the song, and it became about a little independent wooden ship, which developed into *Dreamboat Annie*."

Flicker's production worked wonders, while the musically gifted Leese helped to arrange the songs perfectly. It was, [illegible] say, a match made in heaven. [illegible] first step Mushroom issued the single *Crazy On You* in 1976. The single began [illegible] up the [illegible] heavily in Canadian [illegible] stations, signalling that Heart had [illegible] arrived and – it must be said – in some considerable style.

The debut album *Dreamboat Annie*, released in early 1976, was [illegible] received by fans and critics. It mixed folk music with [illegible] much in the same style that Led Zeppelin had pioneered a few years earlier. It possessed a deeply satisfying sound [illegible] showcased Ann's incredible vocal talents set against songs that have [illegible] test of time.

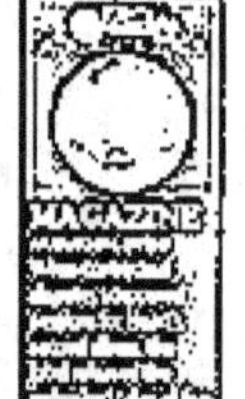

www.ingramcontent.com/pod-product-compliance
Lightning Source LLC
Chambersburg PA
CBHW051927250726
48659CB00002B/880